For God, who sa
darkness." Has shone in our hearts to give the
light of the knowledge of the glory of God
in the face of Jesus Christ.

But we have this treasure in jars of clay, to
show that the surpassing power belongs to
God and not to us.

2 Corinthians 4: 6-7

REFLECTIONS
OF PILGRIMAGE
7 week devotional

DONNA REED PAYNE

Contributing Editor:
Rev. Wren Clanton

Management Editor, Art Director and Graphic Designer:
Elizabeth Bell

Editors:
Elizabeth Bell, Rev. Wren Clanton, Sarah Barbre,
Emma C. Bailey, and Mark Hovezak

Scripture Texts:
The Holy Bible, English Standard Version ® (ESV ®)

If you are interested in purchasing crosses please check out AGORA. They are a Christian based company out of Georgia and can be found online at www.crossinmypocket.com.

Let light shine
out of darkness—
love one another!
Donna Payne

This book is dedicated to:

My daughter and son-in-law, Jennifer and Charlie and
my beautiful grandson, Garrett Reed.

In memory of my dear friend from
another generation, Billie Hiblar.
(Orchard Park Retirement Home, Bellingham, Washington)

In memory of the sweet kind spirit of Shelia Long Garlen, who stood
in awe with us on Rialto Beach, Olympic Peninsula, watching God's
glorious handiwork as the sun set on the Pacific Ocean.
(Pilgrimage 2015)

You will seek me and
find me, when you seek me
with all your heart.
Jeremiah 29:13

God Breathes

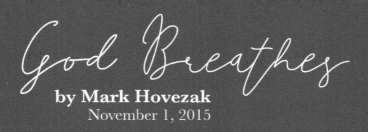

by Mark Hovezak

November 1, 2015

In cozy warmth...and ethereal light,
a fresh cool breeze tenderly stirs.
God breathes, swirling the air.
Lives flutter like leaves, twirling, exhilarated.

Gently guided, our spirits navigate life's plains and valleys
in surging and ebbing flux. Meandering currents
fuse us and then part us anew, as though rough waters were
settling with His light reflecting from life's innumerable ripples.

The vital sinews of our souls are interwoven with others
into vigorous tapestries. Quiet symphonies swell
and glide in hidden harmonic melodies suffusing intermingled
spirits, just as celestial light bathes majestic landscapes in
glorious mosaics of heavenly pigment.

Our souls seem to become inscrutable firmaments,
but God knows what He is doing. Will we listen for that
"still small voice" where immeasurable and
"refreshing" rewards accompany the hearing?

Will we forfeit our option of self-realization and "do" instead
"the will of God", when that destination lies beyond our own
capabilities and senses? There is assurance of His ready assistance
and limitless eternal joy and meaning on that path.

Look up, set your mind on the Lord and on His holiness.
Pray. Listen. Breathe in God's breath and set your feet in
motion according to His Word. You will soon see His joyful
response and be amazed at what He will do.

:her texts used, but not specifically quoted include Deuteronomy 4:29; 6:4, 6:18; 8:3; Jeremiah 29:11-14; Proverbs 8:17; Galatians 5:25; James 1:22, 4:8

pilgrimage:
a journey with
a spiritual intention.

CONTENTS

For God, who said, "Let light shine out of darkness." Has shone in our hearts to give the light of the knowledge of the glory of God in the face of Jesus Christ.

But we have this treasure in jars of clay, to show that the surpassing power belongs to God and not to us.

2 Corinthians 4: 6-7

INTRODUCTION

I want to share God's love for others more than anything. The positive people and experiences in my life: family, hurch, education, career; along with poor choices, broken elationships, and health battles have molded me into who I m. It took a long time to get here and it was not always easy. I elieve God engineered all of it to help me be prepared for this ilgrim's journey. In everything that happened, every ecalculation of my plans, divine foundations were laid for what would be able to do for the Kingdom. I did not get to be the ay at home mom with a large family as I had wished, but was lessed with my daughter, Jennifer. She is an inspiration to me. he's a constant example of God's love and kindness. I taught reschool, kindergarten, and first grade for 28 years. Since etirement I have been engaged in teaching junior high and high chool youth, some of whom I actually taught to read. I love eing immersed with young people and at the age of 64, I feel ke a "seenager".

While in worship at my home church of Huntsville First nited Methodist, I heard Rev. Dr. Glenn Conner preach on a unday in August of 2014. His message resounded on the theme f offering an apology to those you have wronged in the past, no natter how long ago it had been.

He said, “You never know what they may be going through and your apology might just be a blessing to them”. I thought about that statement as I walked to my car. I heard the Lord say, “find your first high school sweetheart and apologize to him”. In high school I had done something unkind that caused us to break off our relationship. It made no sense at all, I had regretted that foolish teenage behavior for 46 years. I had never apologized to him. After some effort, I was able to locate him in Bellingham, Washington and apologize to him.

It was amazing that God had connected us despite a separation of nearly five decades and 2,066 miles. We had each experienced many trials in life and were both grounded in our love for the Lord. We became reacquainted as friends and prayer partners. He also introduced me to a beautiful new place - Washington's Pacific Northwest Coast. For me, being accustomed to the agrarian south and Appalachian foothills, the abundance of glacier topped mountains, rich green rainforests, evergreen islands, rocky beaches, crystal clear streams, salmon, whales, and eagles in the Northwest was a marvelous and refreshing experience. Prior to this introduction, I had merely thought of Washington as a tiny piece of a children's United States map puzzle. When I heard of the astonishing beauty of the area I began researching and before long I was hooked! I started thinking of **pilgrimage.**

PILGRIMAGE: A JOURNEY WITH A SPIRITUAL INTENTION.
-Rev. Wren Clanton

Artist Point
t. Baker Highway

In the summer of 2015, I planned my first pilgrimage adventure of the Washington Coast to visit my old friend and his family. During that time, I went on my first whale watch voyage through the San Juan Islands, made many new friends along the way, and met up with some girlfriends from Alabama to tour Seattle and the Olympic Peninsula. On that trip I took 50 small metal crosses to share along the way. In just four days they were all given away.

In October of 2015, I began planning a very special trip as my family struggled with my mother's declining health, which resulted in her death that December. I needed something to look forward to in the new year. So, I planned a pilgrimage of faith. I prayed for this pilgrimage to open doors for me to travel and share God's love. Having been in the Pacific Northwest for a short time in the summer of 2015, I decided to return there and spend the summer of 2016. I sought restoration for my mind, body and soul. I also wanted to be more intentional about sharing my love of our Savior, Jesus Christ, with people in ordinary places as the Holy Spirit led me.

Seeds were planted for me on that first journey. I returned for another two-month pilgrimage in 2017. The Lord led me to share 400 crosses in 2016 and 600 in 2017. On July 28, 2017, I chose to re-affirm my baptism at Lake Padden through the fellowship of Christ the King Community Church in Bellingham, Washington.

I have felt the promptings of the Holy Spirit to reach out and talk to people. I may meet with them five minutes or two hours. I have experienced the Lord's guidance in sharing how God used me to reach others at key times and circumstances.

I have been blessed to share the stories with many groups and as a result I have been encouraged to write those stories down.

My purpose in sharing these stories is not to highlight myself, but to encourage others to see how we are empowered to let God's love shine brightly through us. Envision two clay pots, one perfect and solid. The other with many cracks and holes in it. Each vessel has a small lit candle inside. A perfect vessel won't shine that brightly, the light reflects back onto itself and up. The broken and cracked vessel shines bright light through every crevice radiating every angle. We are all broken in some way. It is in our brokenness that we can connect with others in authentic love, compassion, and relationship. If you open your eyes and really look at people around you, you can sometimes see their pain, their struggle. You can look past the facade others put up for protection and find the underlying current of their reality.

It is my hope and earnest prayer that this book of stories and scripture, are an invitation for you to reach out to others and to intentionally inspire and empower you to do more, right where you are.

This weekly devotional will include the following components:

scripture
pilgrimage stories
prayers
weekly application
journal space for your own reflections

I invite you to be a pilgrim with me on this journey of reflection, prayer, and outreach.

You are the light of the world. A city set on a hill cannot be hidden. Nor do people light a lamp and put it under a basket, but on a stand, and it gives light to all in the house. In the same way, let your light shine before others, so that they may see your good works and give glory to your Father who is in heaven.

Matthew 5: 14-16

Pastor and family at Deception Pass

a time for
reflection

Prayer

I am devoted to You, God, because of your great love for me and all the many blessings you have showered me with over my life. Devoted faithful savior, I want to pass your love to others . Help me, God. Amen.

Weekly Application

This week bless those people who have been active in your life to nurture and guide you by reaching out with acknowledgement and affirmation through a note or phone call.

Journal Entry

Journal those you contacted and how you reached them. What are your hopes and expectations for this study?

Billie hosting
Orchard Park
ice cream party

Sweet friends at
Jimmy's Personal Care
Fairhaven

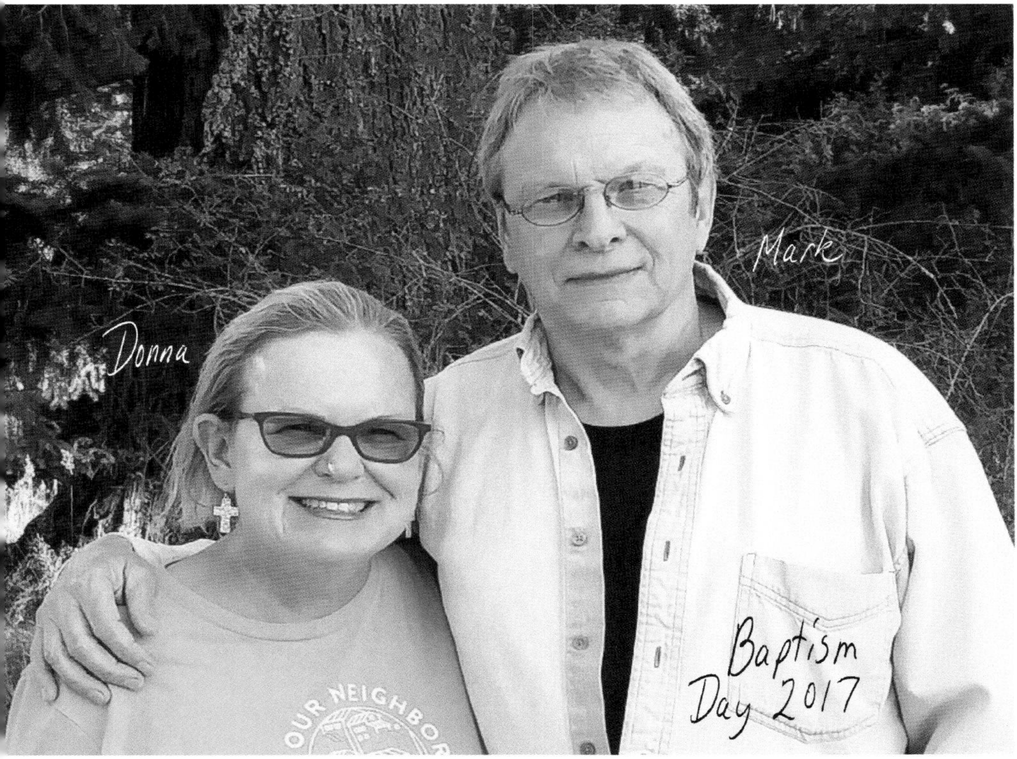
Mark
Donna
OUR NEIGHBOR
Baptism
Day 2017

Finally, Brothers, Rejoice. Aim for restoration. Comfort one another, agree with one another. Live in peace; and the God of love and peace will be with you. Greet one another with a holy kiss.

2 Corinthians 13: 11-12

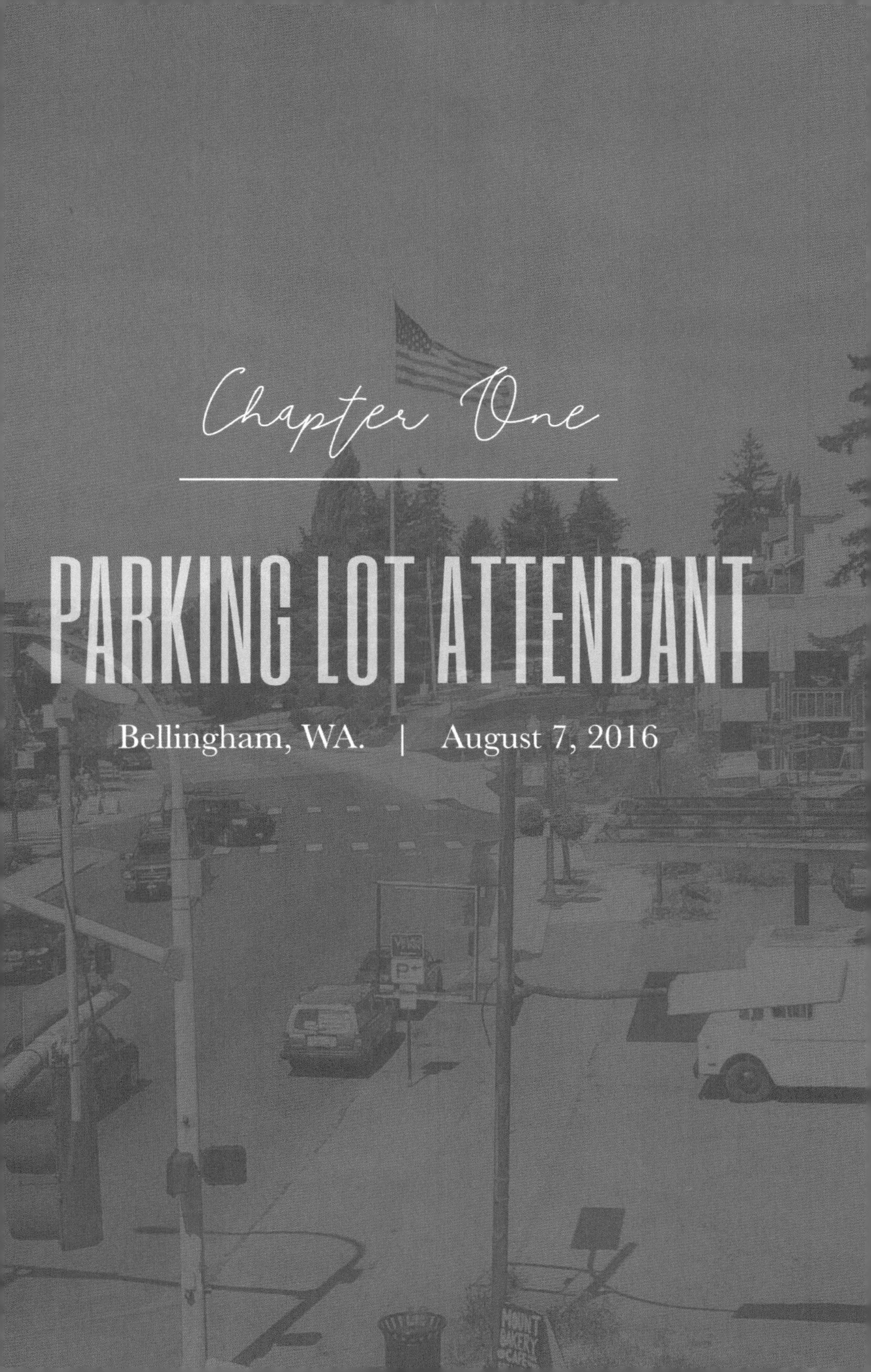

Chapter One

PARKING LOT ATTENDANT

Bellingham, WA. | August 7, 2016

Don't you just love when the Lord speaks to you so clearly through scripture that you feel like you just received a personal text message? The scripture 2 Corinthians 13: 11-12 was in my devotional passages this particular Sunday afternoon.

After church, I decided to go to downtown Bellingham for lunch at a quaint spot called, The Brandywine Kitchen. After eating, I browsed downtown and went into some of the shops to talk and visit with people working in the stores. I shared crosses wherever I went and they were accepted with gratitude. The hot dog vendors on the street welcomed my greeting, brief conversation, and were surprised as I offered them a cross, "God bless you, thank you!" was their response.

But it was the parking lot attendant that remains foremost in my mind. He was standing at attention dressed in full uniform across the street from the Mt. Baker Theatre. A large event was taking place that Sunday afternoon. The skies were gray and a soft rain drizzle fell but not enough to warrant an umbrella. As I passed the empty parking lot, the man stood there almost invisible and deep in thought. Displaying no emotion, I thought, "He must be so bored, so lonely, just standing present like a statue." I almost walked past him. Then I felt the nudge of the Lord. I could not pass this man like he was invisible, like he didn't matter so I turned around to face him and said, "Sir, may I give you this?"

As he reached out to take the small metal cross engraved "God Loves You", I saw a change in his countenance. I saw his eyes soften and tears glisten in the corners.

Ever so gently he put his arm around my shoulder and just kissed ny head. I don't know what his worries and concerns were that lay, but the Lord knew. Maybe he was just praying and ısking; "God are you there?" I felt I was the messenger to espond to his prayers that day and to remind him, that he was 1ot alone or forgotten.

Sometimes we need affirmation. We want to be ıcknowledged as present. We seek the assurance that our life natters and that we are not invisible. It is important to take these noments and make a difference.

Prayer

My Lord and Savior, I pray that You will let your Holy Spirit reside in me and let me see others through Your eyes. Guide me Lord, to see those who are unnoticed and invisible. Help me to see the outcast or bystanders that others pass by without a word, smile, or greeting. Let me shine Your light of love on them in a way that reflects my love for You Lord. Help me to be a messenger of grace to them. In Jesus's name, I pray. Amen.

Weekly Applicatior

This week look for an opportunity to go out of your way tc acknowledge someone who is standing alone - looking invisible. invite you to make the effort to cross the room, street, grocery, o classroom to speak to a lonely person. Acknowledge th neighbor, service worker, civil servant, or anyone who usuall goes unnoticed. Be gracious, be kind, be respectful. Just a smil and a greeting can go a long way

Journal Entry

Post the date, then describe your encounter including who, where and when. What was the person's response? How did it make you feel? How long did it take? What thoughts were going through your mind before and after?

a *pilgrim* on the path.

Kelly - Deception Pass Park

Behold, the former things have come to pass, and new things I now declare; before they spring forth I tell you of them.

Sing to the Lord a new song, His praise from the end of the earth, You who go down to the sea, and all that fills it, the coastlands and their inhabitants.

Isaiah 42: 9-10

Chapter Two

MAIDENS BY THE WATER

Boulevard Park

Bellingham, WA. | August 23, 2016

Having been in Bellingham since June 27, I was missing my only child and dear daughter, Jennifer. Since she had moved with her husband back to Huntsville we had only been apart for a few weeks at a time. Living around the block from them and sitting together weekly at church keeps us connected. But this was a full summer over 2000 miles away. She was coming to see me for a week and I was determined to show her the natural beauty of the area. I wanted to show her the rivers, the sea, the mountains, the islands, the wildlife and especially the whales.

On this particular day, Jennifer and I chose one of my favorite spots, Boulevard Park, which boasts a beautiful large park area on Bellingham Bay complete with a coffee shop and a two-mile boardwalk. It is a hot spot for walkers, runners, picnics, skating, biking, skate boarding, parade of dogs, and wildlife. There is constant activity and opportunities to enjoy being outside in the beautiful sunshine.

While we were enjoying the park, Jennifer noticed some ducklings down at the water's edge and walked down to the shoreline to get a better look. I sat down on a park bench just to enjoy the moment. That is when I heard the singing of a familiar tune of praise music.

I spotted three beautiful young ladies in front of me singing. They were having fun taking pictures of each other and re-arranging their hairstyles. I was drawn to their singing, their smiles, and their radiant countenance.

an Juan Islands

"You look so pretty, let me take a picture of all three of you". I stepped right up to the group and as I took the pictures we talked, shared our faith, and I gave them crosses. It was as if we had always known each other. Jennifer came up and took pictures of us together and we exchanged phone numbers.

Faith, Christina, and Kasey were all active in their individual churches through youth programs and missions. They were not only beautiful but delightful fun-loving girls. We shared the love of Christ. They encouraged me to come back and work with youth programs in that area and asked me to stay in touch with them. It was a blessing the Lord brought these young ladies to me.

I have been involved in communication and meeting with Faith and Christina for several years now. These amazing young ladies teach, encourage, and listen to me as I share the stories of an older "seenage" woman's life. I am honest about how the Lord has carried me through the good and hard times of life. We learn from each other and pray for each other. What a divine opportunity I had to make new friends in Christ.

a time for
reflection

Prayer

My Lord and Savior, I pray that You will let Your Holy Spirit reside in me and let me see others through Your eyes. Guide me Lord to acknowledge those living good and faithful lives in their everyday walk with You. People, young and old, involved in blessed endeavors also need encouragement and affirmation Lord. Let me shine Your light of love on them that reflects my love for You Lord, that I might be Your messenger of grace to them. In Jesus's Holy name, I pray. Amen.

Weekly Application

This week open my eyes to notice young people, even if you are a young person. So much fanfare is made over the accolades of the strong athelete, the star student, the great debater and the best looking kid; but what about praise and acknowledgement for the most important attribute, good character? Look for the young person who strives to be the peacemaker, the caretaker of others, the good sport, the consoler of broken hearts. Call them out and give them a high five

Journal Entry

Note your date and then describe your encounter including who, where, and when. What was the person's response? How did others around you respond? How did it make you feel? How long did it take? What were your thoughts before and after?

pilgrims on the path.

Let brotherly love continue. Do not neglect to show hospitality to strangers, for thereby some have entertained angels unawares. Remember those who are in prison, as though in prison with them, and those who are mistreated, since you also are in the body.

Hebrews 13: 1-3

Chapter Three

RUTH IN THE WOODS

From my prayer journal

Padden Creek Trail | Fairhaven, WA.

July 28, 2017

It was a beautiful morning. I decided to walk the Padden Creek Trail to enjoy the early coolness of morning. As I walked, I asked God to prepare my heart for those I should meet. I was not disappointed. There is always someone who just needs to receive some loving kindness from a stranger. Timing is essential. Many times I had walked this trail and stopped at the Fairhaven Labyrinth to pray, using this ancient prayer tool to focus my thoughts on others. But today was different.

I felt God's nudge to pass by the labyrinth and walk on deeper into the wooded fern filled trail. I went much further than I had been before. The broad graveled path was sheltered by a wooded canopy. The sounds of a brook rang out. The air was clean and fresh and I felt God's breath on me. As I walked further up, the path became smaller and the trees became more dense. When I came to a turn in the path I spotted her - a black woman covered in blankets laying on top of suitcases and belongings. She was clearly homeless. Images immediately flashed to my mind of the news of torment and persecution that women in Africa often endure due to their tradition and patriarchal culture.

As I walked towards her, she lifted her blanket over her head and laid down to hide from my approach. I went to speak to her and gave her one of my little metal crosses, engraved "God Loves You." Surpised, she took the cross and thanked me for it. "Can I pray for you?", I asked. She shook her head no and lowered her eyes. Wishing her well, I continued walking down the path thinking about our short interaction.

Duddy + Me
Nooksack River 2017

As I continued to walk down the trail, I knew that when I returned I would meet her again. What could I do Lord? I had no food with me, just my water bottle and five dollar bill in my backpack. I resolved that I should go back and at least give her the little bit of money for something to eat, perhaps a sandwich and a drink. I was prepared to do more for her as the Holy Spirit led me. The dense trees made the path darker until I made a turn to the clearing where I saw her again. Light was filtering down through the canopy shining right on her as she sat erect with a large worn Bible open in her lap.

As I came closer I could see that it was open to Genesis. "You are reading your Bible!" I exclaimed with excitement growing. "It is all I have," she told me - smiling now. I offered her my hand to shake and introduced myself. She graciously accepted the money I handed her. It seemed that it had been awhile since someone had offered to touch her or see her as valuable. I could see the beautiful woman emerging as we now began to talk to one another. I told her how beautiful her smile was as I noticed she was wearing necklace pendants that looked like symbols of Christian saints.

She mentioned that she had once met someone from Alabama at a Christian conference. I asked where she was from and she replied, "B.C.", British Columbia, Canada - just north of Bellingham. But I suspected from her accent that she was perhaps from Africa or Haiti. She would not explain to me why she was there nor give me her name. I didn't want to impose. I asked, "May I call you Ruth?" "Ruth?", she repeated. "Yes, Ruth. It is a name from the Bible." She agreed while smiling broadly her radiant smile.

he agreed while smiling broadly her radiant smile. I felt that the ord brought that name to my mind and that she needed to hear . "Ruth, may I pray for you?" She agreed and we held hands here together in the woods. I prayed to the Lord, for her rovisions of food, shelter, safety, and for her journey. Prayer was fted up for guidance and for the opening of the right doors for uth.

When I had finished, Ruth broke into the most beautiful pontaneous prayer for me. It moved and surprised me. How ouched I was to receive this gift of prayer in return.

She thanked God for my call to mission and pilgrimage hat led me to stop, speak, and fellowship with her. She broke off nto a language which I had never heard, but I understood that he more than blessed me in prayer. As we bowed in deep prayer nd focus on God, I could feel the presence of passing hikers, ven walking dogs, who had to have witnessed us but did not nterrupt us. They were silent witnesses to our prayers and I pray hat this vision touched their hearts. As we spoke our goodbyes o each other and hugged I felt as if I had just met Jesus, in the voods. I was in awe of that moment and uplifted. It was not ntil later in the day, during my Bible study, that I came across cripture that stunned me. I realized it was Ruth's last words to

Every good gift and every perfect gift is from above coming down from the Father of lights, with whom there is no variation or shadow due to change.

JAMES 1:17

Ruth: a woman of great importance in the Old Testament. She held the attributes of godliness, purity, humility, honesty, faithfulness, and thoughtfulness. Despite great adversity and darkness in her life, she maintained her belief in God and became part of the genealogy of Jesus Christ. What a perfect name for this dear woman in the woods!

a time for
reflection

Prayer

My Lord and Savior, I pray that You will let Your Holy Spirit reside in me and let me see others through Your eyes. Lead me Lord to look in areas where before I might have wanted to look away or avoid. Give me a heart of compassion to see how those who are neediest could have been me or someone I love. Lord, give me Your eyes to see them as a son or daughter. I trust that this is how You see us, Lord, and nothing can take away Your love for us. Lead me, Lord, to shine Your light of love on them that reflects my love for You, Lord. That I might be Your messenger of grace to them. In Jesus's Holy name, I pray. Amer

Weekly Applicatio

This week I encourage you to seek out an area where you fe comfortable and safe to reach out to a homeless or needy perso and offer your time and fellowship, offer them prayer, respec and understanding. Sometimes others just need someone to tal to about their journey, to come alongside them for a bit. You church probably offers volunteer options in a safe environmen Remember that these individuals often feel untouchabl invisible, and unworthy. There are among them veterans th made huge sacrifices to protect our country, some who have lo everything due to catastrophic illness, job loss, or abandonmen Whatever their story, it could be our

Journal Entry

ost your date and then describe your encounter including who, here, and when. What was the person's response? Did you feel at you helped them in some way and how? How did it make u feel? How long did it take? What were your thoughts before d after?

So if there is any encouragement in Christ, any comfort from love, any participation in the Spirit, any affection and sympathy, complete my joy by being of the same mind, having the same love, being in full accord and of one mind. Do nothing from selfish ambition or conceit, but in humility count others more significant than yourselves.

Philippians 2: 1-3

Chapter Four

BEAUTIFUL BELLE

Boulevard Park | Fairhaven, WA.
August 24, 2017

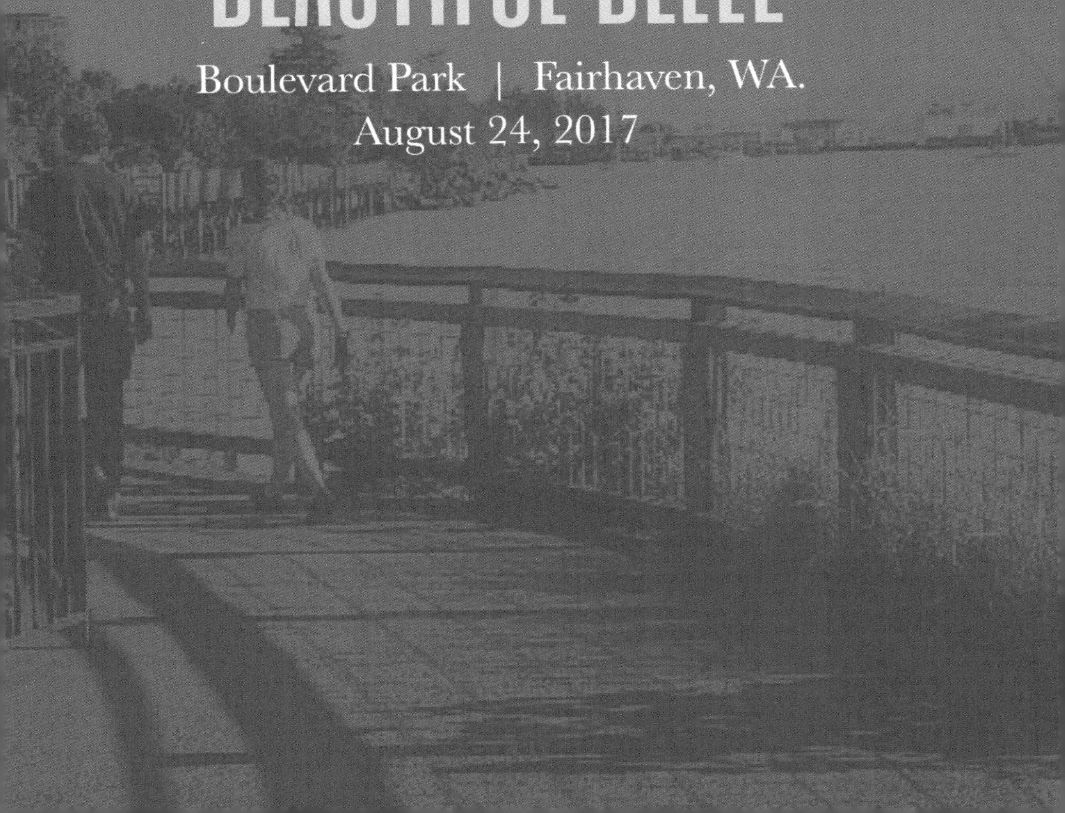

While on summer pilgrimage in Bellingham, one of my favorite evening walks is down the boardwalk at Boulevard Park. It sits at the shoreline and crosses the water of Bellingham Bay. From there you can see the most gorgeous nightly lavender and tangerine sunsets, interact with people and their four-legged buddies, come upon melodic minstrels just casually entertaining those passing by, and marvel at young people biking, skateboarding, or diving off the bridge into the deep water below. The cool breezes are refreshing and I love to breathe in deeply as I walk up the steep Taylor Avenue boardwalk and through the dense blackberry grove to historic downtown Fairhaven Square. This route guarantees about a two mile hike one way with wonderful vistas of boats, kayakers, animal life, and the star attraction of the park area, Woods Coffee. Those who live there year round treasure the long summer days of late sunset, bright blue skies and sunshine.

Most days my walk ends with something warm to drink and a good book in hand to sit and watch the end of a beautiful day. The staff at Woods Coffee knows me well as the one who shares crosses and often brings a new friend in to have coffee and visit.

Some of my
friends at Woods Coffee
Jeff

often engage people in conversation through their pets, taking heir pictures, noticing something nice about them, or just a hello, how y'all doing?". Clearly not from the area, my southern wang easily starts a conversation. "Where are you from?" they sk, "How long have you got?" I wink and then just share ALABAMA!

This particular day I had walked and enjoyed several neetings and conversations, during which I kept noticing a eenage girl. She passed me several times looking sad. She stared traight ahead and walked briskly as if trying to escape some motion welling up in her. Each time she passed I looked for omething to help me engage her in conversation, but I couldn't ind it. Then as I was headed for Woods Coffee to relax and read he passed me for the fourth time.

That is when I heard the Lord say, "Go now, go speak with ier!" But I didn't know what to say till God nudged me again, go NOW!" I turned around walking quickly and then almost an to catch up with her. *"Excuse me, excuse me, miss!"* I couldn't get ier attention, and then I realized she had on earbuds. I tapped ier on the shoulder and she turned quickly to face me. *"You ook so sad, are you okay?* I asked. ***"No, I'm not!"*** she said crying. reached in my pocket and pulled out the little cross engraved God Loves You" and handed it to her. *"Does this help?"* ***"YES!"*** he exclaimed. We hugged while she cried right there in the middle of the busy boardwalk, not caring who saw. *"The Lord sent me o you just now. Can I pray for you?* ***"Yes!"*** *"My name is Donna, what is our name?* ***"Belle."***

"Belle, what do you need? ***"It is just friends and family problems"***, she cried. So we held hands and I prayed for her needs and peace. Afterwards she smiled for the first time and heaved a big sigh, ***"I feel so much better!"***, she explained. We were right next to a bench so I invited her to sit down and talk with me. As this sixteen year old high school girl shared with me about school and her interest in music I began to see a beautiful smile emerge. We sat on the waterside patio enjoying conversation about life. I shared about my teaching career and she about her hopes and dreams. We talked about her getting plugged into a local church youth group where she could use her musical talents in worship ministry and find new friends in faith. The beautiful sunset began to fade and I asked:

"Belle, where is your car?" She had walked from downtown Fairhaven, two miles back on the boardwalk. I realized she had a long walk and it was getting dark fast. Even though I had already had my evening walk, there was no way I would let her go by herself. *"Come on, I'll walk you back to the downtown lights."* As we walked on into the oncoming dusk, you could see visions of people moving but no longer faces.

When we arrived at the blackberry thicket at the top of the hill it was total darkness except for the faint reflection of light on the gray gravel below our feet; we trusted our way from memory. I was so thankful I could walk her into town where she could safely walk in illumination to her car. We exchanged hugs and phone numbers to stay in touch. And then, I turned to retrace my steps through complete darkness. But I knew God was there with me and I was not afraid.

Boulevard Park
Boardwalk
Daddy & Me
Nooksack River 2017

I felt God's shield around me as I knowingly passed dark shadows. It was a walk of faith, I did what God's spirit told me to do, and it was a blessing to me and I hope for Belle too. I walked up the hill in darkness over the railroad tracks and I did not stumble or fall as I reached my car. Relieved, I got in and the first song I heard on the radio as I started the car was Bethel Music's "I'm no longer a slave to fear!" Thank you Lord; I am no longer afraid, and I'm willing to answer your call to help others.

a time for
reflection

Prayer

My Lord and Savior, I pray that You will let your Holy Spirit reside in me and let me see others through Your eyes. Lord open my eyes so I will truly see those with heavy burdens, sadness and despair. Help me see past the mask that sheilds pain and suffering. Help me to set aside some time to slow down long enough to notice, to be available, to be present, to listen, and to show compassion. Lead me, Lord, to shine Your light of love on them that reflects my love for You, that I might be Your messenger of grace to them. In Jesus's Holy name I pray. Amen.

Weekly Application

Many people around us are troubled and sad. We can see this when we take the time to notice. This week choose a place to go where people need cheer and set aside a block of uninterrupted time. Some ideas may be hospital waiting rooms, nursing homes, assisted living, or visiting someone in your neighborhood. Be prepared to take something as a love gift appropriate for your destination: some candy, cookies, a single flower, a cross and offer your kindness of cheer and prayer. Our presence, smile, and cheerful demeanor can lift a hurting heart.

Journal Entry

Post the date, then describe your encounter including who, where and when. What was the person's response? How did it make you feel? How long did it take? What are your thoughts before and after?

a *pilgrim* on the path.

Danie and me
Pottery Party

The Spirit of the Lord God is upon me,
because the Lord has anointed me
to bring good news to the poor;
he has sent me to bind up the brokenhearted,
to proclaim liberty to the captives, and the
opening of the prison to those who are bound;

to grant to those who mourn in Zion —
to give them a beautiful headdress
instead of ashes, the oil of gladness instead of
mourning, the garment of praise instead of a
faint spirit; that they may be called oaks of
righteousness, the planting of the Lord,
that he may be glorified.

Isaiah 61: 1,3

Chapter Five

THE WOMEN AT SILVER LAKE

A favorite trek is to travel to Mt. Baker highway headed to Artist Point in Mt. Baker Park and pause along the way to hike the Nooksack River white water rapids. It is there I feel "peace like a river."

This particular day, I decided to take a side trip off this path to Silver Lake Park. My good friend Billie had mentioned it as a place where her family would meet for family reunions. It was definitely a good place to explore on this beautiful day and in hindsight a definite nudge from the Lord. No sooner had I pulled into the parking lot when two women came walking along the sidewalk in front of my car. As I got out, I called out a greeting to them both.

With my car door still standing open, we all paused and engaged in light conversation. I observed how different they both were in appearance and in spirit right away. Aileen was older and stunningly beautiful, she was tall and thin with long gray hair pulled back and she wore beautiful dainty cross earrings. The younger woman was her daughter, although they didn't look at all alike. Anna was short like me, dressed completely in black. She had obvious scars across her exposed shoulders and arms. Had she been in an accident I wondered?

I shared the little metal crosses engraved "God Loves You" with both women. Aileen and I immediately dove into deeper conversation which Anna impatiently tolerated until she chose to lay down on the ground beside us. We talked for an hour about everything from faith, health issues and the prevalence of depression in young people.

ileen finally came to the point that she felt comfortable to onfide in me and release her burden. Her heart was breaking or Anna. Anna had been fighting severe depression for some me and had been hospitalized, counseled, and medicated. She ad jumped out a window in a suicide attempt. She had tears in er eyes as we hugged several times during her outflow of eelings so heavy on her heart. At that moment she needed a iend, a sister in Christ, to share her concerns, to look into each thers' eyes and talk soul to soul.

It was a divine appointment. Not only did she need me t that moment but she wanted her daughter to witness faith. hey both needed someone to be open, timeless, available, and resent to just listen. As we parted, I turned to gather my things nd to finally close the car door as it had been left open all this me. This meeting took precedence over even shutting the door. did walk on by myself to explore the beautiful park of Silver ake and the wooded paths and walkways. As I gazed across the ke toward the steep mountains, I saw an eagle in broad winged ight across the lake and felt God's presence there.

Oh that you had paid attention to my commandments
Then your peace would have been like a river,
and your righteousness like the waves of the sea;

ISAIAH 48:18

Nooksack River
White water trails

a time for
reflection

Prayer

My Lord and Savior, I pray that You will let Your Holy Spirit reside in me and let me see others through your eyes. Guide me Lord to have the right words and actions that may bring a moment of comfort to those who are mourning personal losses in life or in death. Lead me Lord to shine Your Light of Love on them that reflects my love for You Lord, that I might be Your messenger of grace to them. In Jesus's Name I pray. Amen.

Weekly Application

Reach out to someone who has been mourning a personal loss, maybe in death, or maybe in life. Many have lost loved ones to diseases or to the captivity of addictions. Both can steal loved ones just the same. Offer your sympathy and compassion and a block of uninterrupted time. This invitation involves the gift of time, time to be present and listen. A small gift of a flower or food is nice to bring. We are not able to change what has happened, but for the moment you may bring some comfort to those that mourn.

Journal Entry

Post your date and describe your encounter including who, the situation, and their response. Could you relate to their pain in your life? Did you see a way to follow-up with this person? How did you feel? Did you learn something from them? What are your thoughts before and after?

a *pilgrim* on the path.

Mary Jim with me
Port Angelos 2016

Be kind to one another, tenderhearted, forgiving one another, as God in Christ forgave you.

Ephesians 4:32

You did not choose me, but I chose you and appointed you that you should go and bear fruit and that your fruit should abide, so that whatever you ask the Father in my name, he may give it to you. These things I command you, so that you will love one another.

John 15: 16-17

Chapter Six

THOMAS AT DONOVAN PLACE

Fairhaven, WA. | July 2, 2017

My goddaughter Emma and I were settling into my summer home, a studio apartment in Bellingham, Washington. Exquisite dahlias, snapdragons, and sweet peas were displayed in vases. Bouquets of color were in pots and the small beds surrounding my front door. I love to plant flowers to make even a temporary home feel special and welcoming, welcoming to me and to my guests who will surely come. For me, the fun is in the choosing, planting and watching it flourish. While Emma and I were outside in the parking area preparing flower pots, we noticed a small entourage walking down the sidewalk right next to us.

There was a "punk" looking young man walking a beautiful large German Shephard as two delicate preschool girls walked beside him. Emma, who loves animals, yelled out "I love your dog!" In response the young man stopped and came over smiling so we could pet his dog. He wore slouchy clothes, one ea studded with a large diamond, and was listening to loud rap music. He talked to us between drags on a cigarette. As we petted the dog and spoke to the little girls, I began to look closer at this young man.

I noticed that beyond his tough façade, there was a beautiful young man with a bright smile, sparkling blue eyes, and the most gorgeous eyelashes I have ever seen. Emma and I offered him a small metal cross engraved "God Loves You" and then the walls came down. He turned the music off and extinguished his cigarette. Thomas explained that the dog was his service dog helping him to cope with debilitating depression and anxiety attacks.

July 4th Whale Watch
Emma & Rachelle

He got to spend some time with his daughters when he was okay. He was able to work now because of his well-trained service dog. We discussed the problems of depression that are so prevalent with young people and how the Pacific Northwest's winter veil of darkness further inhibits people fighting this illness.

While Emma played with the sweet little girls, I inquired if Thomas had a church home. I was excited to find out he had attended one of the branches of Christ the King Community Church that I attend while in Washington. He had not been recently due to work schedules, so I encouraged Thomas to attend the Saturday night services or check out the weekly sermons offered online. I had heard one of the pastors there give a sermon about his own battle with depression and how to reach out for help.

I encouraged Thomas to go and seek this Pastor out for advice and encouragement. It was a sweet exchange of fellowship. A Southern "seenage" woman, a teenage girl, a young "punk-rock" father, two little princesses, and a giant German Shepherd. We made a very odd-looking group! We had taken a few moments for kindness, compassion, and to share the love of Jesus while planting flowers, on a sunny day, in a parking lot.

a time for
reflection

Prayer

My Lord and Savior, I pray that You will let Your Holy Spirit reside in me and let me see others through Your eyes. Pride. Lord help me drop my sense of pride to be humble and ready to accept others that are not a mirror-image of the way I look, talk, act, worship, work, or vote. We should respect one another despite our differences. Help me Lord to know the right words and actions that will bring down the walls that separate me from loving others as You have told me in Your Word. Lead me Lord, to shine Your Light of Love on them that reflects my love for You Lord, that I might be Your messenger of grace to them.In Jesus's Name, I pray. Amen.

Weekly Application

Do you have regrets of past behavior? Have you judged someone unfairly, acted on that judgement either to exclude or belittle them? Have you held a grudge against someone for their words or actions against you? The words for this week are kindness and forgiveness. Ask forgiveness or offer your apology – graciously. Bringing down the walls on either side can provide blessings you can't even imagine. Restored relationship is the goal. Make a plan to make a phone call or write a letter or better yet do it in person

Journal Entry

Post the date and describe the situation including who, what the situation was, what course of action did you take, and their response. What was the outcome? How do you feel now? What would you do differently? What are your thoughts before and after?

Trust in the Lord with all your heart,
and do not lean on your own understanding.
In all your ways acknowledge him,
and he will make straight your paths.

Do not withhold good from those to whom it is due, when it is in your power to do it.

Proverbs 3: 5,6,27

Chapter Seven

TIE DYE SOCKS

Fairhaven Village Green
Fairhaven, WA. | August 24, 2017

My sweet young friend Christina and I had just enjoyed a wonderful breakfast at Tony's Coffee Shop in downtown historic Fairhaven. Finishing up a fresh salmon omelet and fresh brewed aromatic coffee, we decided to walk down to the Farmer's Market on the Village Green. The market was bursting with vendors of all kinds; fresh produce, cu flowers, pastries, artwork, handmade jewelry, freshly made meal and a large booth of tie dyed clothing. Just imagine the sights and smells and the sounds of minstrels entertaining as children tumbled and played on the wide green lawn central to this courtyard under a crystal blue sky and radiant sunshine. Everyone was talking and greeting their friends amidst a bevy of colorful market stalls. It was a perfect day in the Pacific Northwest and everyone was out and about and enjoying it.

Having grown up as a teenager in the 60's-70's, I was drawn to the tie dye rainbows and mixed hues. The vendor was tall, robust, and friendly man who greeted us warmly as we overlooked his hand-dyed creations. As we talked I offered him one of the crosses engraved "God Loves You." This opened the door to more conversation and sharing of our faith. He was amazed that I traveled from Alabama to Bellingham each summer. I kept going back to look at some very soft bamboo tie dyed socks that were for sale. I really wanted a pair to give to my daughter. I offered to pay Mr. Harold but found out he was only able to accept cash or check.

I was near the end of this pilgrimage and was very short on cash, depending on my credit card, and I didn't carry any checks with me.

"Well, I guess I will have to pass on this purchase today." Mr. Harold thought a minute and went over to retrieve a piece of paper. He wrote his name and address on it and handed it to me "You take the socks and mail me the money when you get back to Alabama," he said with a big smile. "It will be a few weeks before I get there and get it mailed back to you, it takes awhile tc send mail across the country." "No, you take them! Thanks for the crosses. God bless you!" Both Christina and I were amazed! "That never happens," she said and I agreed. Trust, complete trust, and friendship with a stranger. The only connection between us was our love for Jesus Christ. Whenever I wear thos comfy bright turquoise blue and sea green socks, I think of Mr. Harold and what an impact his witness made on me. Those sock exude pure trust and love, the love of a Savior.

a time for
reflection

Prayer

My Lord and Savior, I pray that You will let Your Holy Spirit reside in me and let me see others through Your eyes. Lord give me the opportunity to encourage someone with my faith and trust in them, even though they have not earned my trust in the past or even if I don't really know them. Let me have a forgivin and gracious spirit, Lord, to know that I have been given much grace and forgiveness from You. I know, Lord, that I can ask your forgiveness and the slate is washed clean. Thank you for the gift of Your Son, Jesus Christ, that makes this freedom from sin available to me. Lead me to shine Your Light of Love on others that reflects my love for You, that I might be Your messenger of grace. In Jesus's name, I pray. Amen.

Weekly Applicatio

This opportunity may not present itself this week or even nex week, because you can't seek it out. It will choose you at som time and at some place. Sometime in the future, you will hav the opportunity to show faith and trust in someone. Pray abou it, watch for it to happen. It may be an opportunity to rebuil trust in someone who hasn't been trustworthy…to give ther another chance to prove themselves. If it is a stranger you trust you may never know the outcome. It will be a witness of you faith in that person and a seed planted. Give God the glory ir your trust, so that you are a witness to God's love for us

Journal Entry

Write your prayers for this opportunity to grow in faith. When you have your encounter, date and describe the event. How did the person respond? How did you feel? What were your thoughts before and after?

pilgrims on the path.

Connie + Danny
Bellingham Airport

WHAT'S NEXT?

How can you show love and gratitude to others just in everyday, ordinary life?

It's not hard to do.

encourage
respect
be generous
acknowledge
smile
forgive

hug
comfort
listen
affirm
pray

Offer a simple cross that says
God Loves You.

The loving kindness you offer,
always comes back to bless you.

A new commandment I give to you,
that you love one another: just as I have loved you,
you also are to love one another.

John 13:34

pilgrims on the path.

Emma at
Boulevard Park

Emma + Savannah
Forks Twilight Museum

Sweet Kay with the family horses Emma and I got to ride ☺

Daddy and Charlotte
2017

Diane and mother
eating out in Lynden, WA
She carried the same cross